WALKING NORTH MULL

by

Olive Brown

and

Jean Whittaker

STANDING STONES, BALISCATE

Brown & Whittaker
2006 ninth edition, revised and expanded.

Trap Landscape

Calve Island and Sound of Mull

ISBN 978-1-904353-09-6
© Olive M. Brown and E. Jean Whittaker, 1986
Brown & Whittaker Publishing, Tobermory, PA75 6PR
Printed by Nevisprint Limited, Fort William

CONTENTS

Public Road	▬▬	Dun or Fort	※
Route of Walk	• • • •	Fence	┼┼┼┼┼
Cairn	△	Gate	┠─┨
Bridge	⊐⊏		
Coniferous Trees	⌖		
Deciduous Trees	♉		

A CODE FOR MULL

1. Gates: Farmers say that when walkers cross their land, gates cause more problems than anything else, so we would ask, on their behalf, that you respect these rules: If you find a gate open, leave it open. If you find a gate closed, shut it after you again, securely fastened and stockproof. If you find a gate locked or tied up with string or wire, please don't try to open it. Climb it at the hinge end.

2. Dogs: Dogs also cause problems for farmers so we would ask you to keep your dog under control where there are animals, and to take special note of the lambing season (March - May) when you should not walk amongst sheep at all. The bond between the ewe and her new born lamb can be permanently broken if they are disturbed. If you find any animal in distress such as an apparently lost lamb or a sheep stuck on a ledge, report it, do not attempt to deal with it yourself.

3. Deer: North Mull is not stalked on a regular basis but the dates for the stalking season should always be borne in mind. The stalking season in Scotland starts on 1st July, though there is little serious work until August. The season then continues until the middle of October. If in doubt, take local advice.

4. Go carefully on single track roads. The passing places are for vehicles to pass or to allow overtaking. Never park there or any where it is likely to cause difficulty of access to farmers' fields.

5. Respect wildlife, wild plants and trees and guard against fire. On Forestry Commission land, respect F.C. Bye-laws, 1992.

6. Leave no litter. Build no unnecessary cairns!

"Know the Code" countryside access leaflets available from Tourist Information Centres.

Keep your dog under control, Trig Pillar, Speinne.

INTRODUCTION
Where can we go for a walk?

Prompted by this frequent request for suggestions, we published the first edition of this guide. As we go to press with this ninth edition, we feel we have been to some extent successful in answering the question. Revisions have been regularly made and new walks added. All the walks remain only suggestions, as the whole of Mull offers great scope for walking. *Walking in South Mull and Iona* is a companion volume offering a similar variety.

Unique to all islands, but particularly so to Mull with its 300 miles of shoreline is the sense of the encompassing sea. With one exception, the sea features in the views on every walk and is, perhaps, the most outstanding aspect of walking in any part of Mull, affecting the quality of light for artist and photographer, giving always a sense of space and freedom and, in clear weather, a prospect of distant islands away in the west.

Each walk has been thoroughly explored by the authors, and a sketch map of the route as well as a description has been included. Taking along the Ordnance Survey "Landranger" map of the area (Sheets 47 and 48) would be an asset and the three "Explorer" maps sheets 373, 374 and 375 cover Mull at a larger scale. Grid References are given where necessary and heights are quoted in metres. The Ordnance Survey's spelling of Gaelic place names has been adopted as a matter of convenience. In the text, the word 'route' has been used for the direction taken, even where there is neither path nor track. One of the greatest pleasures of Mull is that the walker is so often finding his own route away from recognised paths and tracks.

We must thank the farmers and landowners over whose land you will pass. Their co-operation and helpful suggestions have been invaluable.

If you have a car, thought should be given to where you park it while you are walking. The passing places on single track roads should not be used as this could impede traffic. Try to pull off into a roadside quarry or onto a patch of firm ground. Like most of the Highlands, the peaty soil of Mull is very boggy and it is best to wear sturdy footwear. A wind and waterproof jacket is also advisable. The time suggested for each walk allows for steady walking but no allowance for stops has been made. As the authors tend to linger, watching birds, pottering around deserted villages and exploring caves, the times may be thought to err on the generous side, but it should always be remembered that a mile of route finding over heather moorland is a much longer mile than a mile along the beaten track. We hope that this little book will make the route-finding that much easier.

Tobermory   **Olive Brown**
August 2006   **Jean Whittaker**

1. The Lighthouse Walk

Fairly easy walking but can be muddy in places in wet weather.

This delightful short walk begins right from the main street in Tobermory. From the lifeboat shed behind the pier at the eastern end of the street, take the path that slopes gently uphill. The way follows the coastline about 50 feet above the shore, at first winding through woods. Look out for wild garlic in summer and hazelnuts in the autumn, and possibly the sleek dark heads of seals in the water. The path then opens out and slopes down towards the lighthouse. The lighthouse was built last century and first lit on 10th November, 1857. Just over a hundred years later, in 1960, the light became automated and the lighthouse keepers' cottages have passed into private hands. This was part of the progressive automation of all Scottish lighthouses and today none are manned.

Nearby is the memorial to Robert John Brown, son of Archibald Brown, who founded Browns shop in Tobermory in the mid-nineteenth century. It has a useful panorama identifying landmarks in a wide circle including Ben Hiant and the village of Kilchoan across the Sound of Mull and peaks of Rum visible to the north-west. Beyond the lighthouse the shore curves away in the long sweep of Bloody Bay, site of the sea battle in 1480 when the waters ran red with blood.

The return can either be made by the same route or by scrambling up the steep path directly above the memorial on to Druim Nead an Fhirein (hump of the raven's nest). Follow the path south-east till the golf course fence is reached. Walkers cross the course at their own risk. Go over the stile and follow the path marked by the green topped posts keeping strictly to it. To the east and south are sweeping views of Calve Island, the Sound of Mull and Ben Talaidh. After the path drops steeply down through a patch of trees, it keeps close to the perimeter fence until it reaches the gate. Follow the path towards the town, turning left at the War Memorial down a stepped path to finish at MacBrayne's Pier.

Lighthouse and Ben Hiant

2. Aros Park

Aros Park serves as a public park to the inhabitants of Tobermory. It is now managed by Forest Enterprise. It is a place to enjoy the rhododendrons in the spring, to fish in the ornamental lake in the summer and to pick brambles in the autumn. At any time of year it is pleasant to wander in the policies of the former Aros House and to take a short walk down to the old stone pier where the puffers once brought supplies for the big house.

If you wish to walk to Aros Park, there is a path along the shore from Tobermory, giving enjoyable views of the bay and the town. Start at MacGochans pub in Ledaig car park, Tobermory. The path gradually rises and levels out above the sea. At the top of the steep section there are beautiful views over Calve Island which forms a sheltering barrier across Tobermory Bay. Follow the path as it descends steeply back to sea level, across the wooden bridge and up to the open area once the site of the mansion, Aros House (demolished 1962, but see picture on page 10). This route originally connected the big house with the town, and MacGochans pub at the beginning of the walk incorporates the old lodge house.

To reach the park by car, leave the Tobermory-Salen road about a mile out of town where Aros Park is signposted. Go through the white gates and follow the drive down to the car park where there is an open grassy lawn where the imposing mansion of Aros once stood (demolished in 1962 but picture on page 10). This was once owned by the Allan family of the Allan Shipping Line which ran from Liverpool to Canada. There are picnic tables and toilets at the car park and a circuit may be made of the loch on a path which is well signposted and level. The loch is full of water lilies, both white and yellow species, and is surrounded by trees and rhododendron bushes, making it pleasant and sheltered. Forest Enterprise have done a lot of work clearing the former paths and overgrown areas, and have cut down large areas of *Rhododendron ponticum* which was threatening to overwhelm more unusual rhododendron species and other shrubs. They have put up boards giving maps and information about aspects of this Victorian estate.

Having completed the tour of the loch, the return to Tobermory can be either by the same route or by following the main driveway as far as a stone bridge. Here there is a signpost to the Upper Falls. These falls, with a direct drop of about 40 feet and a long run of white water at their foot, are spectacular after heavy rain.

Continuing on this path brings you out on the main Salen-Tobermory road, at a small car park, and there is a footpath back to the park gates or all the way back to Tobermory.

On the way back to Tobermory, a short detour can be made up the lane between the small industrial estate and Baliscate House. About a quarter of a mile up this track are two standing stones. with a third lying flat between them. These are thought to date from about 2000 BC and are among quite a large number of standing stones in north Mull.

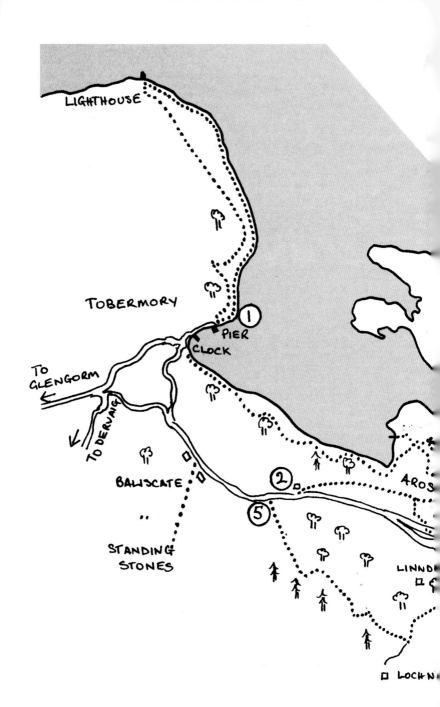

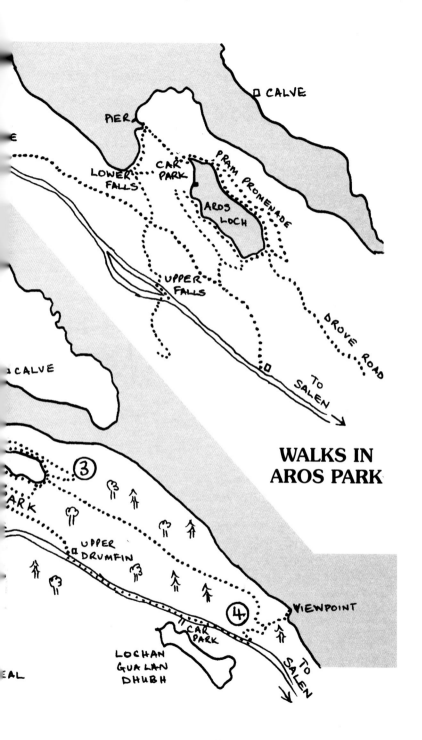

CALVE

PIER

LOWER FALLS

CAR PARK

PRAM PROMENADE

AROS LOCH

UPPER FALLS

DROVE ROAD

TO SALEN

CALVE

WALKS IN AROS PARK

③

ARK

UPPER DRUMFIN

④

VIEWPOINT

CAR PARK

LOCHAN GUALAN DHUBH

TO SALEN

EAL

9

3. Pram Promenade

This is a walk long overgrown and forgotten except by a few who could recall it from their youth, including someone who can remember being wheeled along this scenic path in her pram. Alas, you would have difficulty in pushing a coachbuilt pram along it today. When it was created though, it was a sunny promenade for the children of Aros House – a place to look out over the mansion and its grounds and across the bay to distant Tobermory.

Aros House

From the north end of the loch, cross the dam and a little way along the lochside path a flight of steps leads up into the trees gradually gaining height until it becomes a fine level promenade looking down onto the loch. This continues the length of the loch until you reach a fallen beech tree – stoop under the twisted boughs and follow the path passing a huge old larch on your left. The path zigzags down the hill then swings right to take you back to the lochside. If continuing on to the Apper Mor track, look out for a small path at this bend which takes you steeply down to the track.

4. Apper Mor – once an old drove road.

3 miles 2 hours

In the eighteenth century, one of the biggest cattle markets in the Western Isles was held in Glen Bellart on Mull (see page 36). Cattle from Morvern on the mainland which were destined for this market were ferried across the Sound of Mull and landed on the area of drying shallows between

Calve Island and Mull, where the boats could be beached and the cattle driven ashore easily.

The remains of a building, reputed to have been an inn providing refreshment for the thirsty drovers, may still be found close to the high water mark. From here the cattle were driven up to attain the highest point on the Tobermory-Salen road at the Gualan Dhubh (Goolan Goo). The first part of this ancient route is traceable only with extreme difficulty since conifers have been planted over it, but a good track exists between the Gualan Dhubh back to Aros Loch, and makes a pleasant stroll through a mixed woodland carpeted with mosses. These mosses are of such splendour and variety as (almost) to compensate for the damp Atlantic climate which is the reason for their exuberance and luxuriance (wellingtons recommended!).

Leave the Salen-Tobermory road where Apper Mor is signposted and drive down to park in the marked area. The first part of this walk is on a firm forestry extraction road, with fine views across to the Morvern shore and Drimnin House. At the point where the forestry track goes sharply uphill ahead of you, take the old and rather muddy track to your left. This part of walk is through a shady stretch of mature woodland mixed with planted conifers until you reach the loch side. Now you are in Aros Park and can follow the path round the loch in either direction until you come to the main car park. From here make your way up the main drive to a sign to the left to Upper Drumfin. This driveway leads up to one of the three lodges of the former Aros House, now the home of the Mull Theatre company. From the lodge gates you are a mile along the footpath to the starting point.

Sound of Mull and Ben Talaidh.
This splendid viewpoint now takes some finding since the track was rebuilt, but it is possible to reach it by following the line of the burn at the first bend after the car park. Standing on the edge of a rocky volcanic dyke that runs out here, you look south-south-east down the Sound of Mull to Ben Talaidh and beyond. The red buoy marks the wreck of the Hispania, *a Swedish cargo ship which sank in December 1954. Sport diving is very popular in these waters and this is one of the most spectacular wrecks in Scotland.*

5. Burgh Boundary to Linndhu

Another walk in the Tobermory area – this is popular with dog owners: no road and no sheep. It is also popular with riders, so be prepared for the path to be churned up by hooves. Nevertheless it is a very pretty walk through mixed woodland with rather secret glimpses back to Tobermory Bay and out over the Sound of Mull.

As the start of the walk is less than a mile from Tobermory town clock, it is quite possible to walk out along the road. Leave the Tobermory-Salen road a few yards beyond the coloured signs that mark the old burgh boundary where there is a rough track. If you go by car, park on the verge of the main road at the entrance to this track. Walk into the track and almost immediately turn uphill to the left. The whole of this broad ridge is criss-crossed with paths – go quietly and you will probably see some of the deer which make them. The variety of the woodland – larch, spruce, broadleaves and old coppice make this an attractive area to wander through, but it is more a place for patient exploration than brisk walking and wellies are undoubtedly better than boots. With a certain amount of persistence it is possible to work your way through, keeping to the high ground, and get out onto the Loch na Meal track that leads to Loch na Meal farm. It is then possible to return to Tobermory through Aros Park which makes an interesting circuit. Once on the Loch na Meal track, turn left and walk down to a wooden house, turn right, then left at the main road. Cross over to the car park and head for the river. A roar of water soon advertises the presence of the Upper Falls, one of the splendours of Aros Park. Follow the river down till the path meets the main driveway. Once you are down into Aros Park you can choose from the various possibilities shown on the map on pages 8 and 9.

Old Stepping Stones, Ledmore.

6. Circuit of Loch Frisa   *13 miles, an all day walk*

Part of this walk may be closed when sea eagles are nesting – check for information about visits to the hide.

This walk takes you right round the shores of Loch Frisa, the largest loch in Mull. The route suggested is a complete circuit of 13 miles, but the less energetic pedestrian may prefer to lay on a pick-up vehicle at one end. This secluded loch is rarely glimpsed by the motorist, but the tracks around it serve the walker well. Done as a whole, it provides a day of steady tramping in one of Mull's most restful landscapes. The sea is far away and the countryside is undramatic. The harsh forces of volcano and ice that carved the landscape of South Mull are muted here and where the walker expects to walk along a valley he finds, instead, that he is walking in a basin with the loch keeping its distance and the hills of South Mull remote on the far rim.

Just past Loch Torr on the B8073 (Tobermory-Dervaig) road there is a new bridge with space nearby to park, such as on a part of the old road beside the old bridge. This is still a difficult corner and cars must be parked well clear. Walk towards Dervaig and, just past the first post marking a passing place, strike off left through the gate. This soon becomes a walkers' track, offering quick and easy walking towards Loch Frisa, although it will be fully an hour before the loch comes into view, with the shapely cone of Ben Talaidh in the distance.

Follow the track until it goes into a forestry plantation by a gate. The loch can be seen through the trees with the ridge of Speinne Mor on the far side. Half a mile out of the plantation, when the conspicuous promontory on Loch Frisa and the Lettermore farm across the water are in line and there is a cairn on a ruined building at the side of the track, drop down off the path and work your way towards a gateway in an old electric fence. This short stretch is hard going through heather and bracken but will be covered in 10 or 15 minutes. As you follow the contour round the loch side of the small hill there are various rough tracks which merge in a track to Tenga Farm. Before the farm is reached the track goes through a gate and on your right you will see some standing stones given their Gaelic name of carrachan. Only four stones are visible and though someone has put iron stakes marking where a circle could have been, no conclusions can possibly be drawn without expert excavation.

From here, continue through another gate and make for Tenga farm buildings, identifiable by some tall conifers growing behind them. It is necessary to go through the farmyard so extra care must be taken to close gates and keep dogs under control. Turn sharp left at the end of the farm buildings and take the track which goes up and over the hill. As it goes over the top, there is a gate. Pass through this and follow the line of electricity poles towards the Ledmore river.

Formerly the only way across the river was by string of large stepping stones. However, a bridge now carries you safely across the river. Passing through two gates walk up to the forest road. It is now possible either to turn right and make for the Salen-Tobermory road (2 miles) or left to continue the circuit down the east side of Loch Frisa. Felling will be in progress from time to time in the area as part of Forest Enterprise's harvesting and planting cycle. Warning signs must be observed. Just before Lettermore Farm the road divides and the walker should take the right fork as it goes uphill. Continue on this road high above the loch, occasionally stopping to look back for fine views towards Ben More. Near the head of the loch there is a gate and a little further on a jetty and the shore buildings of a fish farm, including a house and garden. The slope to your right leads up to the Bealach Naithir the Pass of the Snakes – because of the area's reputation for adders. At the main road, turn left to return to the start.

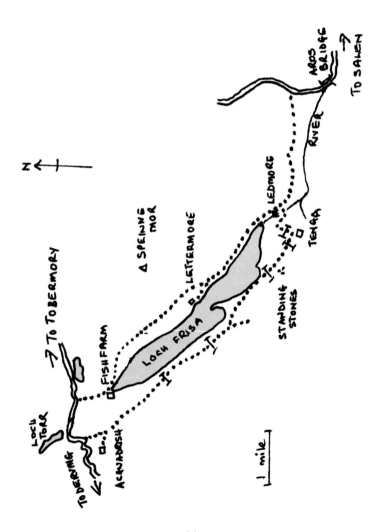

All the motorist sees of Loch Frisa.

7. Speinne Mor

444m

Ascent from Mishnish Lochs   *302m of ascent, 3½ hours*

Alternative circuit by Loch Frisa   *7½ miles, 5 hours*

Speinne Mor is the highest hill in North Mull. When viewed from the upper part of Tobermory its ridge and summit form the south-west skyline above the tree-clad slopes of the bay.

The ascent is a straightforward walk (see map, page 18) up the northwest ridge from the Dervaig end of the Mishnish Lochs. The top loch, Carnain an Amais, takes its name from the funeral cairns now submerged in the heather, that marked the resting place for the coffin bearers on the way to the burial ground at Kilmore above Dervaig. Just as you go down the hill after the top loch, there are convenient quarries for parking. The walk starts at the larger quarry. Go over the stile at the back and follow the ridge tending always to the right until the iron posts of an old fence are picked up (note that in mist these posts are an invaluable aid to descent). Follow this fence along the Loch Frisa side of the hill enjoying a good view of this, the largest loch in Mull.

When Lochan Dearg comes into view away to the left, the walker should abandon the posts for the steep slope to the left which will take you up to Speinne Mor's imposing summit cairn – comparable only with that on Ben More and designed to protect the surveyor at the Ordnance Survey trig pillar.

Return by retracing the ridge or by descending to the shores of Loch Frisa. Set off from the summit down towards the loch aiming for the distinctive promontory on the opposite shore, and keep this course until the edge of the trees, at first fairly steep but becoming less so approaching the field above Lettermore. At the bottom of the field, turn right along the forest road and follow the last part of the Frisa circuit. See page 14.

Loch Frisa from Speinne

Speinne – view from the summit

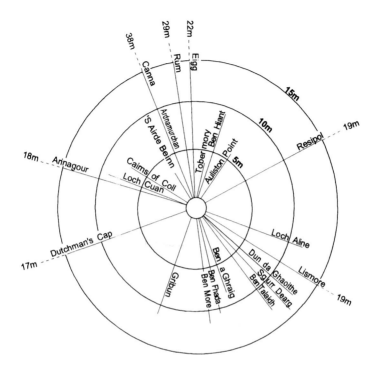

8. S'Airde Beinn or Crater Loch

295m   958ft   1¾ miles, 1¼ hour, 140m of ascent

This popular short walk affords maximum reward for minimum effort and the finest view in north Mull from the top. Hidden away in the crater is a dark and secret loch.

Start 3 miles out of Tobermory on the road to Dervaig (B8073) at the ruined cottage which is on the right hand side halfway along the Mishnish Lochs. Go over the stile out of the parking place and follow the path behind the cottage, crossing another stile further up. From here the rim of the volcanic crater is in clear view. This rim, always steep and on its north and west sides entirely precipitous, is broken only where the burn emerges. Tend always to the right, aiming for the notch on the horizon, gradually getting closer to the wall and the burn, until you break through the crater rim. Cross the wall and the burn and make for the first cairn on the crater rim.

From here a half-hour walk in an anti-clockwise direction completes the circuit of the crater walls, with time to admire the view from the north cairn. This cairn is not actually the summit – the highest point is about two-thirds of the way along the west rim. Follow the path down the steep descent to the moorland plateau, covered in Bog Asphodel in June, back to the start.

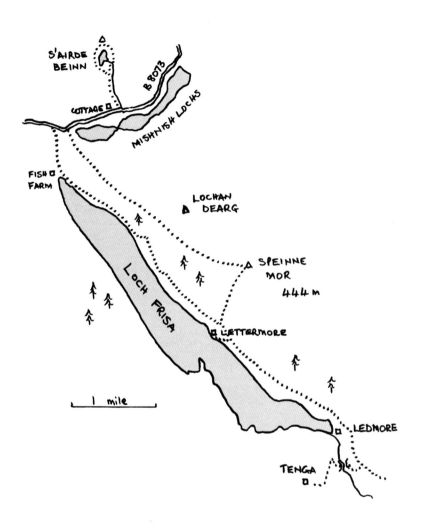

S'AIRDE BEINN

B 8073

MISHNISH LOCHS

COTTAGE

FISH FARM

LOCHAN DEARG

SPEINNE MOR

444 m

LOCH FRISA

LETTERMORE

1 mile

LEDMORE

TENGA

9. Cnoc Fuar

This is hardly a walk at all but ideal for some brief brisk exercise on a winter's day when the ground under foot is very wet.

The start is two miles out on the Glengorm road from Tobermory. Park your car near the cattle grid and walk up the private metalled road to the array of communication masts for radio, television, British Telecom, Northern Lighthouse Board and emergency services. As you reach the top, a wide view of the Sound of Mull comes into sight and, as you look back, the hills of north Mull can be seen. The hill is called Cnoc Fuar – the cold hill – often a very apt name.

10. Cill an Alein   *less than a mile*

This is one of the best of the short walks that Forest Enterprise have waymarked and has an interesting objective. The old graveyard of Cill an Alein has a variety of old gravestones dating back to the middle ages, though the earliest legible inscriptions date from the eighteenth century. One of the most intriguing, a small stone near the bottom of the graveyard, commemorates a shoemaker who died in 1742. On the back of the stone is his hammer and a stylish high-heeled shoe of the period.

Start at the car park beyond the Forest Enterprise offices which are at Aros Bridge on the main road just north of Salen. The route is waymarked and can be done in either direction. The graveyard is in a clearing about half way round and views over Glen Aros can be enjoyed from it and from the several seats along the way.

There are other short walks waymarked by Forest Enterprise at Fishnish, Garmony and various other places throughout Mull – see page 47.

11. Salen to Killiechronan

7 miles, 4 hours

(or Mull coast to coast!)

These two routes can be combined into a circuit. Both Aros and Killiechronan are places of much greater antiquity than Salen. In the early nineteenth century, travellers for Staffa would land at Aros, and cross over this neck of land to take ship on the Atlantic coast of the island.

Leave the car by the jetty just beyond the 30 m.p.h. limit on the Tobermory side of Salen, being careful to allow access to the sea. Walk on towards Tobermory for a few yards and pass through a gate which takes you on to a track which rises gently through mixed woodland with views between the trees over the Sound of Mull and Salen Bay where, near low tide, seals are often to be seen basking on the exposed reefs.

The track leads across the fields to Glenaros House. Follow it all the way to the farmstead where a succession of gates takes you past the farm buildings, bearing left through the last gate by Kate's Cottage where there is a notice "Footpath to Loch na Keal." Once through this gate, keep alongside the wall on your left which runs south and uphill from the farm. Ahead, on the skyline, you can see the remains of a ruined hill fort. Follow the track towards this, fording a burn, the Allt a Chaisteal. The track now

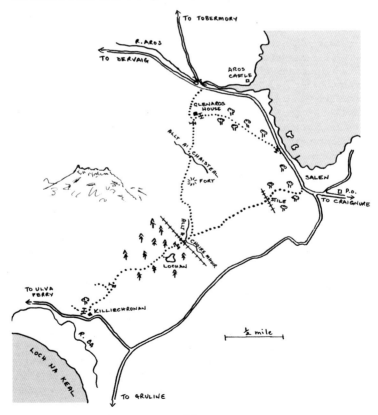

goes to the right of the hill on which the old fort, Cnoc an Sroine stands. The rubble remains are considerable but there are only small sections of constructed wall still left and if you climb up to it there is a good view to the north of Glen Aros and the ruins of Aros Castle at the mouth of the Aros river. To the south you can see the Ben More group and, back from the shores of Loch na Keal, the large white shape of Knock House standing in the trees.

Rejoin the track and follow it as it becomes less distinct and tends downhill to the left, following the line of a shallow valley parallel to and some distance from the forest. After a while, it crosses the burn, the Allt a Choire Mhoir and comes down on a well defined track. Turn right on to this and cross the burn to enter the forestry plantation – a large oak is a marker for the entry point. A gate, a short fenced section and another gate takes you into the wood and a reasonably good path eventually joins an unsurfaced track. At the junction, a stub of road takes you up to a viewpoint overlooking a lochan frequented by ducks. The track leads steadily downhill till it reaches a gate. Once through the gate the track goes straight on and then runs alongside a wall behind Killiechronan House and so out on to the B8073 Salen to Ulva Ferry road.

Starting from Killiechronan to walk over to Salen, leave the road between Killiechronan House and the sawmill, bear right before the old farm buildings (now holiday cottages) and pass through a gate. Then, with the wall behind the house on your right, continue through another gate until the track bends away uphill to the left. At this bend there is a high deer fence. Go through this and follow the route previously described as far as the double gate out of the forest. From here, the choice of routes lies between going back due north or by bearing right in a north-easterly direction after crossing the burn. The open aspect as you walk over the shoulder of the hill gives good views of the Sound of Mull and beyond to the hills of Ardgour. The grass airstrip of Glenforsa stands out just beyond the last houses at Salen. The path drops down now through birch woods and reaches Salen near the 30 m.p.h. limit.

12. Beinn na Drise   *An all-day walk, 424m*

The combination of the two ascents of Beinn na Drise enables the walker to retrace an old way over the hill from the sea to Glen Bellart, emerging at the ancient cattle fair of Druim Tighe Mhic Gille Chattain. This market was a gathering of drovers from all over the Western Isles and the adjacent mainland and buyers from the south and from Ireland. Today it needs an immense effort of historical imagination to stand in lonely Glen Bellart and see it thronged with people and animals – to hear the quick exchange of Gaelic and the lowing of cattle. The logical significance of this site at the meeting of drove roads from Ulva, Gometra, Tiree, Coll, North Mull and Morvern demands that we think in terms of travel by sea and the grazing requirements of the cattle. From the market, the cattle were driven to Grasspoint to be ferried to the mainland by way of the island of Kerrera, then on to the trysts at Crieff and Falkirk. The Glen Bellart cattle fair was not just a market place for the black cattle of the Highlands but a gathering of traders, pedlars and entertainers, and for several days three times a year there was an encampment of hundreds of people. This was a social gathering as well as a commercial one and the traditions are in some way reflected in the Salen Show, the annual agricultural show at nearby Glenaros.

To reach the site of the fair, pass through the gate on the north side of the road at the watershed. Note that this gate is a narrow pedestrian gate provided by the Forestry Commission alongside one of their much wider access gates. Beyond is a firebreak some 20 feet wide running in a northerly direction. After about 300 yards there is a small grassy hollow to the right. The rough stone foundations of huts used at the time of the fair can still be found, overgrown with heather and moss, on either slope of this hollow. These low stone walls were covered with branches and turf to make small huts on the hillside while there was good grazing for the cattle in the valley below.

Ascent from Glen Bellart

Park the car on the watershed on the Glen Bellart road. The deer fence is replaced by a sheep fence on the Dervaig side of the watershed and there is a gate where the two fences meet. Pass through the gate (and not over the stile in the deer fence) and walk along the outside of the deer fence, following up the Allt Glen Mhic Caraidh, which tumbles down in a series of little waterfalls and limpid pools. Continue along the fence which bends

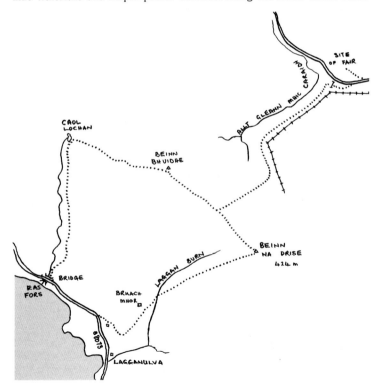

away from the river until the slope steepens and then make for the col between Beinn Bhuidhe and Beinn na Drise, keeping to the drier ground at the foot of the slope. Turn left at the col and climb to the summit of Beinn na Drise.

Ascent from Lagganulva

Park the car half a mile north of Lagganulva Farm just before the road enters woodland. Where the woodland begins, a track leads up to two cottages and then out onto the moorland beyond, zig-zagging steeply up the hill about 50 yards from the cottages and leading up to the old village of Bruach Mhor. The village is a little to the left and off the direct route up the Laggan burn. Follow this burn up to its head, then strike off north-east up the slope to your right to gain the summit of Beinn na Drise (meaning 'Hill of the Brambles' though none are evident). From this direction the hill is a series of false summits, but the highest point (424m) has an Ordnance Survey trig pillar surrounded by a cairn. From here, in the distance, you can see (looking south and turning clockwise) Ben More, the Gribun cliffs, the Ross of Mull, the Treshnish Islands, Quinish Point, Speinne Mor, Loch Frisa, the Sound of Mull, Lochaline and a glimpse of Loch Ba. At your feet lies the island of Ulva.

Ridge Walk to Beinn Bhuidhe.

For the walker with a car at Lagganulva, the ridge walk to Beinn Bhuidhe offers a fine upland walk for striding over the moorland away from recognised paths and tracks. From the top of Beinn na Drise set off across country towards the next high point. Beinn Bhuidhe (387 m) which means 'Yellow Hill.' This is splendid walking and there is a good chance that you will see a herd of deer leaping off as they scent your arrival. In the spring you will hear skylarks singing, and there are always moorland birds to be seen. From the top of Beinn Bhuidhe take a WNW course towards Caol Lochan, a narrow loch lying in a hollow. From there, follow the line of the

burn, Allt an Eas Fors towards the sea, keeping far enough away from the burn to avoid one or two deep gullies carved by the course of the water, as these involve awkward scrambling. The burn reaches the road by a series of waterfalls, but the most spectacular, Eas Fors, lies just across the road where it plunges into the sea. From there it is about half-a-mile back along the road to the car, unless you wish to see Eas Fors from below. A hundred yards along the road towards Dervaig, scramble down to the beach and walk back along the shore to stand below the fall.

THE WALKS

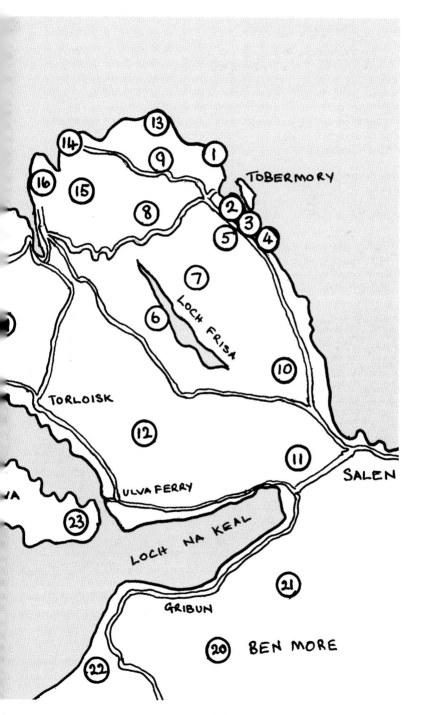

13. Ardmore Forest

8 miles 4 hours

This is a well-known walk, thanks to signposting by Forest Enterprise who own most of the land covered. A reasonably sheltered walk in bad weather, the route can be done in either direction and several variations are possible. Old villages, shore paths and occasional splendid seaward panoramas make this the best forestry walk on the island.

Leave Tobermory by the Glengorm road and follow it for 3 miles to the car park signposted Courtesy of Glengorm Estate by Forest Enterprise. Park and go through the gate and head down the track. Highland cattle may be grazing here. Go though a second gate into the Forestry land. Scattered all over the Ardmore area are the remains of old buildings and deserted villages and barely 200m from the gate there is one up to the right. A little scrambling over the remains of Forestry felling brings you to the ruined houses of the village, a place called Cnoc Corrach. One of the houses had an interesting example of ship graffiti – this stone was removed for conservation purposes and can be seen at Duart Castle.

Continuing on the track, past an old track which takes off to the left, takes you into enclosed plantation for a while. In a little, though, the view opens up and you can see the view across to Coll and up to Ardnamurchan, the most westerly point on the British mainland. On a good day, especially in late evening, you may see far off in the west the Outer Isles of South Uist and Barra. Following the Ardnamurchan peninsula back inland, the first cluster of houses is the village of Kilchoan with the Ben Hiant ('Mountain of the Fairies') to the east of it.

Follow the track downhill until you see some more ruined buildings ahead of you. Here a path signposted "Shore Path" takes off to the left and you can leave the main track to do a loop down to the shore. The buildings

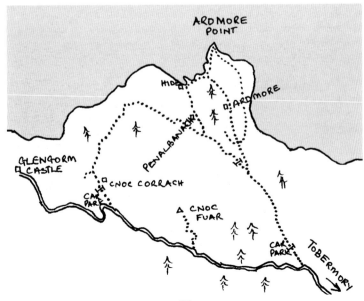

are what remains of Penalbanach. The small buildings have a typical layout of a room either side of the entrance with a smaller back room between them. You can see the sockets for the joists for the upper floor which would have had coomb ceilings. Houses of this type are still found in Argyll Terrace in Tobermory. Behind the main building, which is rather grander, are a series of shedding pens for separating sheep when this was a working farm.

Carry on down the shore path, following the posts. Where the trees begin to thin out it is worth looking ahead to see if there are any seals on the exposed reefs. The stand of Sitka spruce that used to grow in this corner were said to be the fastest growing trees of their type in Britain. Their recently planted successors appear to be doing equally well. Just on the final descent to the shore, on the right opposite a rowan tree, are the remains of what is thought to have been an icehouse. Humble icehouses, built into the hillside like this, were used by fishermen to keep their catch fresh. Down on the shore there is a little hide for watching seals and shorebirds. From the hide, retrace your steps to a red-topped post put where the route continues over duckboards. The route continues, marked by posts, over the rough ground just above the shore, though wooden steps and bridges make the going easier. Wild flowers are abundant on this stretch from May to July. A large cairn indicates where the route goes back inland, but a short excursion can be made to see Ardmore Light.

Ardmore Light detour – this light is visible from eight miles out to sea and is now solar powered. To reach it, follow the shore (rather rough and rocky). The light commands good views of the entrance to the sound of Mull, usually busy with vessels of every sort and size. From the light, climb up to join a good track which rejoins the direct track from the shore cairn.

From the cairn (without the detour) follow the red-topped posts back to the main track. At the top of the first long slope you will pass on the right the ruins of Ardmore, which are very similar in age and appearance to Penalbanach but still deep in the forest and covered in the lime-loving fern Maidenhair Spleenwort. Shortly after this you cross a burn by stepping

Ardmore

stones. Above this crossing are two more ruins, one of these is said to have been the schoolhouse which once had as many as thirty pupils. This may seem a surprising number but the Ardmore area was full of little villages, and more may yet be revealed as further tree felling progresses. The path goes to the left and rejoins the main track.

From here you have the choice of turning right to return to the car park at Glengorm or left to walk directly to Tobermory. The Shore Loop, past the ruins and along by the sea, makes a very pleasant walk done in the reverse direction from Tobermory, parking where signposted just beyond the landfill site a mile out of Tobermory.

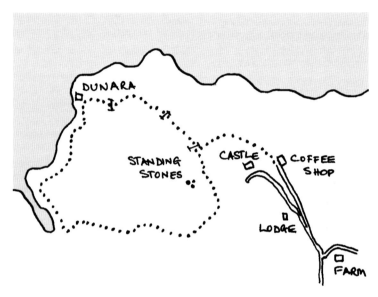

14. Dun Ara Castle, Glengorm   *a half-day walk*

A short walk over farmland to the remains of the medieval castle of Dun Ara perched on top of one of the vertical, circular outcrops which are such a feature of the extreme north of Mull.

Park at the Coffee Shop (signposted) near the castle. Cross a small bridge and follow the track round below the castle until it joins another track above a group of three standing stones. Bear right and follow the wall down towards the sea. After passing through two more gates, look back for a fine view of Glengorm Castle. Now the track curves round to the left and as you go through one last gate you will get your first sight of Dun Ara perched 15m up on top of a rocky outcrop on the right of the track. There are the foundations of two old buildings where you leave the track. A narrow rock gully on the SE side of the knoll leads you easily up through the original entrance. The best part of duns and forts is often the spectacular site – there is rarely much to observe in the way of tangible remains, but Dun Ara, being

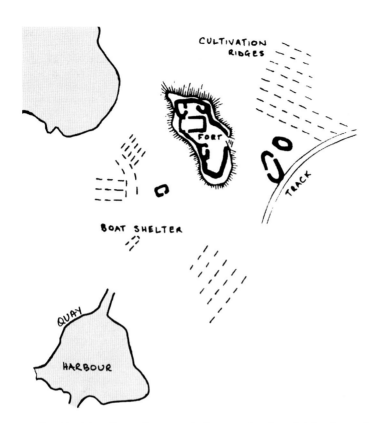

medieval in date, offers rather more in the way of walls and defensive works. The fort watched over the sea from Quinish Point round to the castle at Mingary, which is also medieval. There are the footings of three buildings on top of the rock, and looking down, the remains of associated outbuildings and cultivation ridges may be seen. The castle is thought to have been a stronghold of the MacKinnons. To the SW, a circular pool has been identified as a harbour, with the remains of a small jetty, quay and boat landing. Local tradition has it that this so-called harbour was improved as a bathing pool for the Lithgow shipping family who once owned Glengorm Castle.

The return can be by the same route, but a longer circuit can be made by continuing westwards, keeping to the high ground at first. When a fence is reached, do not cross it but keep it on your left. Go round the left side of a rocky knoll and go down to the tidal inlet, Laorin Bay. There is a small pier which was used to bring in coal and other bulk supplies to the estate in earlier times. To return follow the cart track over the hill and through the trees until you are above the standing stones. Here you rejoin the outward track for a short walk back to the Coffee Shop for some refreshments.

15. Dervaig Back Road

From Dervaig (to which there is a bus from Tobermory) take the first right after the 30 mph sign and go up the road and track until you come to a high gate with adjacent pedestrian swing gate. There is a small car park here. Go through the swing gate. A path to the left takes off into a woodland walk area and you can make your way up through this to cut off the first corner of the forestry road or simply walk directly up the track. After a couple of miles a long straight ends in a long curve and a meeting place of routes. This is the spaghetti junction of North Mull and care needs to be taken to make the correct exit. The forestry track sweeps round the long

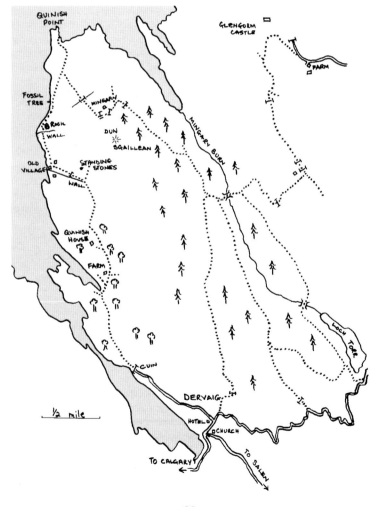

corner and heads straight southwards, but the route of the old road goes straight on, dropping down over the edge of the road signposted for Glen Gorm, Ardmore and Loch Frisa. There are however, other options. To choose one of these, go to **Spaghetti Junction** at the end of this walk. To continue on the Back Road, follow the sign and drop down to the bridge over the Mingary Burn. This takes you to a large turning area where another forestry road comes in from the right. Ignore this and walk across the turning area and out at the track at the back. There is now only another half mile of forest before the road emerges into rather desolate country between low hills. On this stretch there are three farm gates. Please follow the Code for Gates on page 2. Turn left at the junction to walk towards greener pastures and in a little while a jungle of *rhododendron ponticum* advertises that you are approaching a Scottish baronial mansion, built at a time when planting rhododendrons was at the height of its fashion in the West Highlands. Glengorm Castle was built by James Forsyth in 1860 and was at one time owned by the Lithgows of the Clyde shipyard, Scott-Lithgow.

Just before the castle comes in sight there are two hay barns on your right and a track takes off to Dun Ara (see page 28). Keep straight on the road and you will pass about a hundred yards south of the castle to come out on the tarmac Tobermory-Glengorm road about 200 yards outside the lodge gates.

As you follow the twists and turns of this road you are rewarded with delightful views, at first over the sea to other islands (the Outer Isles can be seen on a good day) and then inland over the Sound of Mull to the hills of mainland Scotland. For those with energy to spare, a detour may be made through Ardmore (see page 26) which avoids two miles of tarmac.

Spaghetti Junction
Option 1 a few yards before the back road takes off, another track goes off to the left, heading back at an acute angle. This will eventually take you to Mingary farmhouse and Quinish Point and links up with Walk no.16, returning you to Dervaig.
Option 2 If you continue on the forestry track, you will eventually emerge above Loch Torr. To return to Dervaig from here, involves something of a slog up the hairpins of the main road and over the hill. It is possible, however, to cut off the hairpins by taking a grass grown ride through the forest which takes you out on the last hairpin near the top of the hill. This ride takes off about 200m beyond a long straight where the forestry track emerges from the trees and affords an open view down to the meanders of the Mingary Burn. The track then plunges back into the trees and a few yards further on there is a turning place to the right. The grassy ride takes off at the end of this turning place and its beginning is marked by a small cairn. This is a mossy, green and shady ride. Once all the walks in this forest were like this.
Option 3 From the wide turning space above the Mingary Bridge, a forestry track leads southwards to Loch Torr, crossing back over the burn a little below the Torr dam. The last part of this walk, high above the banks of Loch Torr, is rather fine, but there is no way of short-cutting the hairpins that take you back over the hill to Dervaig. At the top of the hill, in the wood to right of the road, there is a setting of standing stones accessed through a small car park. You may like to stop and visit these before enjoying the fine views over the village as you walk down the hill.

16. Quinish Point *An all day walk*

This is a walk of great variety, covering woodland, farmland, seashore and coniferous forest. A notable feature of the walk is some fossilised trees discovered on the shore by P.A. Macnab in 1984 and described by him in *The Scots Magazine* in March 1986.

Starting from Dervaig village, make your way up the village street, following the road into the country beyond the end of the village, until you reach the entrance to Quinish estate, marked by a high gate. This gate should be shut at all times. Follow the estate track, forking right at each junction until the old farm buildings are reached. Pass straight through the yard behind these, ignoring the track going uphill to the right. The route leads on to pass behind Quinish House, and continues through pleasant deciduous woods and fields of grazing cattle, with the views opening up all the time.

Half a mile past Quinish House, fork left and head down towards the sea. The right-hand fork gives a ten minute diversion to some standing stones on a grassy platform. Only one of these is still erect. After another couple of hundred yards the track is crossed by a wall. Go through the upper of the two gaps in the wall and, keeping the wall on your left, continue towards the sea, passing over a stile by the gate out onto marshland at the bottom of the field. Cross the marshland following the path to the ruined houses by the shore, all that remains of an old village, Ardantairbh.

To reach the fossil trees (half an hour's walking from the ruined village) follow the shore along northwards towards Quinish Point, until the shore route is blocked by a rocky outcrop. Go over or round this and the wall beyond. From here, the hillside ahead can be seen coming down to end in a line of crags. The fossil trees lie below these crags. A marker that you are close to the site is a prominent and odd-shaped rock on a knoll (see sketch). The shape of the largest tree can be seen lying below high water mark, its root system still recognisable and its fallen trunk pointing out to sea. The trees are in a good state of preservation – having been undiscovered for so long, they escaped the Victorian craze for collecting that has left MacCulloch's Tree in South Mull largely an empty shell. The Quinish trees are, in addition, not true fossils. When they were overcome by a lava flow the tree inside rotted, leaving only a mould. This was later filled by a subsequent flow of harder lava and the first lava flow eroded to leave the perfect cast of the tree. A sample of the cast of the tree is no different from a bit of rock anywhere in the vicinity – it is pointless to take anything but photographs. This tree is best visited at low water, but can still be seen except at the highest tides.

The figure in the photograph is seated on the rootball of the tree and the trunk stretches across the bottom of the picture.

Continue towards Quinish Point along the shore for a rather tortuous but attractive route through a rock scenery of dykes and sills. Alternatively, you can head for the point over the moorland top for easier walking. The most southerly of the twin rock bastions that mark the end of the land at Quinish was fortified in the Iron Age, but it is the second headland that is Quinish Point. From this dramatic headland, with the sea boiling at its feet, there is a fine view north towards Ardnamurchan, west towards Coll and south, beyond Caliach Point, to Tiree.

A track curving back round the hill leads from Quinish Point to Mingary farmhouse, now a holiday home. As you pass through a gate in a wall, ahead of you can be seen Dun Sgaillean. Those of an archaeological turn of mind can make a slight detour to visit this other Iron Age fort, the oval outline of its walls just discernible on top of the rocky mound.

When you reach the farmhouse go through the gate (where the notice says 'Forest Walk' and out at the gate at the bottom. Follow the track and then the path over the hill until the corner of the forest comes into view, with the turrets of Glengorm Castle away in the distance. The path goes into the forest between two posts. The path is rather rough and boggy at first, but becomes a well-made track after a short distance and eventually joins a forestry road. Turn right on this and continue through the trees until finally emerging on the outskirts of Dervaig. To return to the starting point, go on down the hill to the hotel and turn right into the village.

17. Langamull

4 hours

One of the best beaches on Mull, with something of interest on the way for all the family. Start where signposted on the B8073 Dervaig to Calgary road just before Mornish (car parking) and walk through the larch forest for about 20 minutes. Here there is another small car park where Kildavie Settlement is signposted. To visit this settlement turn off to the right in to the forest and follow the path marked occasionally by green posts. Notice the banks of coppiced trees on your right – coppicing is a method of timber management where trees are cut down but leaving a substantial stump from which new trunks grow. These can be harvested at any stage depending on the use – thinner poles for wattle fencing, thicker poles for more substantial fence posts or logs for burning, but never left until the trunks are too heavy to manage or might bring the tree down. An ancient tradition but in tune with modern ecological regeneration principles.

Cross the burn by a small bridge, or wade through the ford – look out for the tell tale signs of otters: a dropping or "spraint" left on one of the exposed rocks in the burn marking its territory. Be careful not to miss the path turning to the right into the former village of Kildavie. An ancient settlement of ruined buildings no more than four or five courses high and covered in thick moss. In this quiet and sheltered spot entirely encircled with trees, it is difficult to imagine a busy village with men, women and children going about their daily lives, with hens pecking round the doorways and cows grazing nearby. At the time this village was last inhabited in the late 18th century, there were very few sheep on the island but goats were popular.

Archaeologists may want to linger here, but to continue the walk to the beach, return to the car park and go through a metal gate, down the track

The lost village of Kildavie

and through two more metal gates (for notes on gates see page 2). The track swings to the right now and the walk from here is over firm machair until you reach the dazzling white sand. Langamull is a beach with something for everyone – cosy nooks among the rocks to sunbathe or have a picnic, rock pools to explore – one large pool is filled by the tide but warmed by the sun and is deep enough for a few swimming strokes. The sea gets deep fairly rapidly so serious swimmers do not have to wade out far before getting afloat. Fishing from the rocks is another pastime to enjoy.

For the energetic there is a short steep climb up to a small cairn – the cairn is inside the remains of an ancient dun – and the reward is panoramic views to Coll (only 10 miles away), to Ardnamurchan Point and Lighthouse, and the islands of Eigg, Muck, Rum, perhaps Skye, and on a good day the Outer Isles.

From this cairn walk along the high ground just above the thickets of small scrubby trees. Descend to the rejoin the path between the second and third electricity poles (counting from the beach) as a substantial wall blocks your way, and clambering over it is not advised. Return along the track passing Langamull farmhouse on the left, and back near the wooden gate there is another dun, Dun Mhadaidh high above on a rocky knoll.

Richard Atkinson (recommendations)

18. Treshnish Headland   *8 miles An all-day walk*

This walk can be done as a whole but is divided into three sections: the circuit probably affords the best views of coastal cliff scenery in north Mull. The Ardmore cliffs are more impressive but lie below and out of sight of the walker, whereas at Treshnish, the walker in most places proceeds along the level of the 100 foot raised beach – a sort of corniche for pedestrians constructed by the ancient sea between two bands of vertical cliff. There are also some caves to explore for added excitement. Excitement for the walker, however, is also potential danger for farm animals. The crumbling cliffs of Treshnish present especial hazards and dogs should be put on a lead (or left behind) during the lambing season and kept on a lead where there are cows and young calves.

Leave your car in the roadside car park opposite the passing place 200 yards south of the private drive to Treshnish, and walk down the track to Treshnish Farm. There is no parking at the farm or on the drive. From the house, go left to pass behind the farm buildings and follow the track to the old village of Haunn. Unlike many of the deserted villages of Mull, the houses here are not in ruins but converted to holiday cottages. The track goes on towards the sea cliffs and down to a most attractive shingle bay with a natural rock arch at the far end. The whole of this coast is sculpted with stacks and caves and arches and was used for location shots when *Eye of the Needle* was filmed. Beyond Haunn, the hundred foot raised beach is very obvious and provides broad, level walking to a point a little below Crackaig. Out to sea, the Treshnish islands float in line astern: Cairn na Burgh Beg, Cairn na Burgh More, Fladda (the flat one), Lunga (the highest one) and the Dutchman's Cap. The Dutchman is, at first, hidden by Lunga but draws clear of it as the walker works round the peninsula. Indeed the energetic pedestrian who does the whole circuit in one may see these enchanting islands change formation from being in line astern to being in line abreast. Amongst the many caves which penetrate the cliff is one known as 'The Whisky Cave', the location of an illicit still. The mouth of the cave is partially hidden by a grass-grown mound which was deliberately constructed to conceal the entrance and the operations of the still. A marker for the way down to the cave is the top of the Dutchman in line with the sea-cliff on the south end of Lunga. When this point is reached, descend by a steep, grassy gully to a stony beach. To your right, well tucked into the cliff is the cave. The solidly built foundations on which the distilling tub sat are about 15 feet across. After this deviation, the walk should be continued along the level of the cliffs until, when the cliff on the south end of Lunga is in line with the cliff on the north end of the Dutchman's Cap you will have reached a flat, open area, where there was once a medieval chapel.

The cliffs ahead now look noticeably steeper and the slope below them is clothed in scrub. To continue the circuit you must descend to the shore. If you now want to return to your starting point you should climb up to the deserted villages of Crackaig and Glac Guagairidh (pronounced 'Cookery'). Each village is a scatter of six or seven houses built with rounded corners in

DUTCHMAN'S CAP   LUNGA   FLADDA   CAIRN NA BURG sheltered spots to resist winter gales and rain. Crackaig was inhabited almost within living memory but Glac Guagairidh was abandoned following a typhoid epidemic in the nineteenth century. To walk back to the road, take the path which follows the contour of the hill to the right to avoid the boggy valley floor. A little before the road, you come to a stone house restored from the shell of the old Reudle schoolhouse – a two storey building which children from neighbouring villages attended until about 1870.

This house is the landmark for those wishing to come in on the circuit at this point. There is a grassy area for parking at the side of the tarmac road just north of the private drive. Walk up this drive and about 30 yards before the gate there is a waymarked path to the left. Follow this round the house, through a field gate and the path will take you directly to Glac Guagaraidh. As you cross the high ground before the village the Treshnish Islands come into view with Staffa, a rather box-like outline, away to the left. Beyond Glac Guagaraidh, tucked into a fold of ground on the right, is the second village, Crackaig. To get down to the sea from Crackaig, take the path that crosses the stream, heading away from the village for about 150 yards until the path dips down into an ancient, winding track, obviously designed for the feet of highland garrons.

The next section of the walk is only possible below half tide – consult the tide tables before you set out.

To join or continue the circuit, go down from the level ground into a bouldery bay. Continuing eastwards along a rough and rocky shore with no defined path brings you to another splendid cave some 220 feet deep, 35 feet high and 29 feet wide at the entrance, tenanted by rock doves. Just short of the back wall, the roof comes down to within a couple of feet of the floor and, for those prepared to venture beyond, there is an inner chamber 40 feet long. Assuming that the tide is far enough out, it is possible to continue along the shore and regain the raised beach below

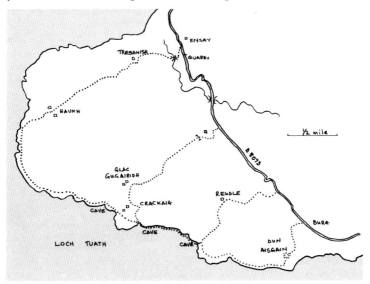

Reudle. If returning to the road past Reudle, head inland up the side of the valley of the Allt Reudle, bearing left at each fork of the path. From the one house that has been restored a good track leads back to the road. This completes the second section of the walk round the Treshnish Headland.

The last section of this walk returns to the raised beach. From the cairn on the shore, go inland for about 200 yards, cross the burn and climb up to regain the raised beach, which provides pleasant and easy walking to the end of the circuit. In early summer Bloody Cranesbill blooms profusely and is one of the sights of the cliff. Across the waters of Loch Tuath lie the

Crackaig

islands of Ulva (visitors welcome) and Gometra. Right at the end of the walk is Dun Aisgain, perched high on a rocky bluff above the ruins of a deserted village. This is a galleried dun, dating from the Iron Age and is one of the best preserved examples in Mull of these fortified structures. Make your way up past the dun which occupies a conspicuous position and has a fine view towards Ben More, dominating the head of Loch na Keal.

Keep on up the hill path to join the road at Burg, keeping above the fence in the valley.

Ben More across Loch na Keal. Note raised beach

A Bird List for Walkers

Any attempt to set down a restricted bird list is bound to be idiosyncratic. The following list is intended simply to be an accompaniment to the walking guide and lists those birds that one might reasonably expect to see on a woodland or farmland walk, a walk by the seashore or freshwater, and a walk up into the hills. In terms of Mull birds there are some glaring omissions – on the Treshnish Islands, puffins gather in their thousands during the breeding season and the ledges are raucous with guillemots and razorbills. But to get these ticks, you will have to give up a day's walking and take to a boat. Nor is this a list for those who can already tell a Willow Warbler from a Wood Warbler or a Sandpiper from a Little Stint. We hope you will be arguing as to whether a Sea Eagle should have gone in and a Hen Harrier should come out, but most of all we hope that you see lots of birds that are not on this list of 60.

Woodland
Blackbird
Finches, Chaffinch, Greenfinch
Hedge Accentor (Dunnock)
Common Wood Pigeon
Robin
Tits, Blue, Coal, Great, Willow
Siskin
Song Thrush
Sparrow
Great Spotted Woodpecker

Farmland
Hen Harrier
Hoodie Crow
Greylag Goose
Kestrel
Lapwing
Pheasant
Common Snipe
Starling
Stonechat
Grey Wagtail
Pied Wagtail

Seashore
Curlew
Black Guillemot
Gulls – Common, Herring,
   Greater Black-backed
Grey Heron
Red-breasted Merganser
Oyster catcher
Redshank

Shag
Shelduck
Wren

Freshwater
Little Grebe (Dabchick)
Dipper
House Martin
Mallard
Mute Swan

Hills and Moorland
Buzzard
Golden Eagle
Meadow Pipit
Ptarmigan
Raven

Summer Visitors
Cuckoo
Common Eider
Spotted Flycatcher
Sand Martin
Skylark
Barn Swallow
Wheatear

Winter Visitors
Goldeneye
Fieldfare
Redwing
Teal
Wigeon
Whooper Swan

19. Kilninian to Calgary

4½ miles 2½ hours

This track called the Crois Mharaidh Dhubh (the Crossing of Black Mary) linked the population of Kilninian and Mornish, and is now signposted by the Scottish Rights of Way Society. A useful walk for those families divided into beach loungers and walkers: if the beach party drops the walkers at Kilninian, the walkers can take to the hill and the whole party can meet up again on Calgary's white sweep of sands.

Leave the B8073 a few yards west of Kilninian Church, famous for its 16th century carved grave slabs, now in the vestry, which include the figure of a man in armour holding a claymore. From the church, a track winds up the hill through the gate and passes in front of a cottage and a caravan. Immediately after, head left up the hill past the spruce trees and out into the high enclosures. At the top of the enclosed ground there is an old wall with a small wooden gate.

From here on, the path is not always easy to find, but you cannot go far wrong by following the picturesque course of the Allt Hostarie, at some distance from it, to a conspicuous bend in the burn. Here you can take as your mark a very distinctive pyramidal hillock on the horizon. The path passes to the right of this and then curves round the right hand edge of a rather undistinguished moorland plateau to reach the summit of the walk at Lochan an h-Earba. Here the view opens up, and the rather restricted southwards view of Ulva and Gometra, with Iona beyond Gometra, is replaced by a broad prospect to the north: Ardnamurchan Point directly over Quinish Point with the Small Isles (Muck, Eigg, Rum and Canna) beyond. On a good day the Cuillins of Skye can be seen in the gap between Rum and Eigg.

The path now follows the Allt Torr a' Bhacain, first through a valley, then high above with some nice airy views into the river bed. Just before a forest fence is reached, there is a ford across another burn with a fine waterfall upstream.

At the fence the old track slants down through the forest heading for its original destination at Mornish School, now a private dwelling but used as a school within the past 20 years. This old track is now obliterated by conifers at the lower end, and it is necessary to cut down through a forest ride to the main road. It should be noted that if the walk is undertaken in the opposite direction, the starting point is now signposted at the large gate in the deer fence and that to make the junction between the ride and the

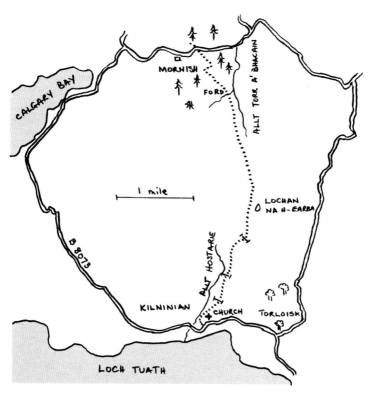

ancient track you must bear right where the ride tends away to the left (waymarked by an arrow ->) and drop down towards a little stream. The old track follows the direction of this little stream uphill.

Once the road has been reached, turn left to follow the road to Calgary bay about one mile, and rejoin the beach party for a well-earned lounge.

Kilninian Church

20. Ben More

966m (3,169ft) 5 hours

Stalking season August to 20th October. Tel 01680 300229

Ben More is the highest hill in Mull and the only "Munro" (a peak over 3,000 feet) in the islands other than Skye, affording a relatively easy climb with the extra sense of achievement of having climbed from sea level. It is a deceptively bland hill in its northern approaches, a steady slog up the first 2,000 feet with all the interesting features back and out of sight, but in the last 1,000 feet the true scale of the mountain is revealed and its dominance amongst the Mull hills is established. To climb from the north take the road west from Salen, park near the bridge at Dhiseag (492359) and go up the path behind the farmhouse which follows the course of the Abhainn Dhiseig. Increasingly splendid views northwesterly to Ulva and the Treshnish Islands, and west to the imposing cliffs of Gribun, relieve the first stretch as does the river on the left hand, punctuated with falls and cascades and, in September, with the bright red colours of the rowan trees.

Often called "champagne summit", Ben More is a place to celebrate birthdays, anniversaries and the completion of the Munros.

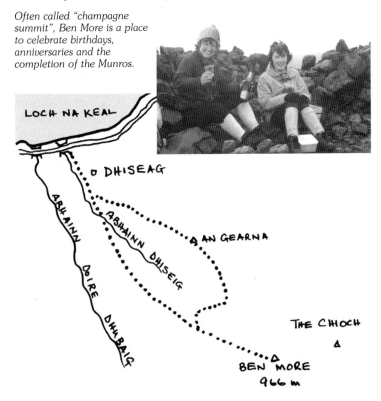

The Chioch from Ben More

At about 2,000 feet, the path comes onto a broad stony ridge with cairns at frequent intervals. Southeasterly winds have a habit of blowing quite strongly and locally across this ridge. After a sharp ascent the summit ridge, with its sheer drop off the north face, is attained. The summit cairn stands at the far end – a circular shelter cairn, welcome on cold and windy days. The summit is in character with the hill – the approach to the cairn is a bland stroll with little gain in height and it is only on looking back that the walker sees the great curving wall of the north face whose top he has just crossed. The summit itself lies within a few feet of the steep drop to the Chioch 150 metres below with all the hills of Mull, hitherto hidden by the bulk of the mountain, suddenly on view in all their barren austerity. Beyond them again, breaking against the eastern horizon like the waves of the sea, are the hills of the Scottish mainland, Ben Nevis lying over the end of Loch Ba. There are not many days when the summit of Ben More is windless enough to enjoy all this splendour to the full. If you are up there on one of them, cherish it. If you are up there on a really good day, you might see Northern Ireland – the faint outline of Errigal, highest of the Donegal hills appearing like an overturned saucer floating on the sea westwards of Islay.

The descent can be made by the same route, or for a change, by bearing right after the first sharp descent and following the contour round to go over An Gearna (563m) with its well-built cairn. This route gives a fine view into the north face of Ben More and the Chioch.

21. Beinn Fhada   *5 hours*   *707 m*

This a fine ridge walk, not only because of its distinctive rocky character, but also because it takes you into the heart of the hills that rise from the southern shore of Loch na Keal. Beinn Fhada is the hill next to Ben More and although not as high, it has perhaps more variety and surprises.

Leave the road between Knock and Disheig just past the bridge over the Scarisdale River. Walk up the hill with the wooded valley of the river on your left – avoid going up the other side as the river splits into two deep gorges. As you come over the lip of the hanging valley work across and then up the slope of the hill which is getting steadily steeper. It will take you about two hours, working upwards through the rocky outcrops, to reach the first summit (marked by a small cairn) which is the start of the main ridge. Stopping from time to time to catch you breath, you can admire the views across Loch na Keal to Kellan. Although everyone seems to pick their own way on the ascent so far, from the cairn follow the clearly trodden path along the ridge. Another fifteen minutes brings you to a tiny lochan, and another twenty to the final pull up to the craggy little summit – not as hard an ascent as it looks from the approach, though some caution is required in conditions of snow or ice. On a clear day the view over to the Chioch and Ben More is spectacular and there are other good views down into Glen Clachaig.

There are several choices from here – return by the route you came up, continue out to the next lower summit, An Cruachan, and down towards Loch Ba (see Glen Clachaig in *Walking in South Mull & Iona*), or work down to the col. From the col, you can go up the Chioch and onto Ben More, but this route should not be undertaken in adverse conditions such as very strong winds or ice underfoot as there is no way off the Chioch ridge. A pleasant way back to the start is the long steady descent from the col through the wide glaciated valley, following the Allt Gleann Fhada. This is a dramatic little river, every so often hurling itself over an edge of rock in a fine waterfall. At about 150m, just below one of these waterfalls, the river splits in two forming an island. On this tiny island are the remains of some buildings, thought to have been an illicit still from the days when there were crippling taxes on whisky. At this point, make sure you are the east bank.

The river saves its biggest surprise for the end of the walk. Only a few hundred yards from the road, the waters are channelled between the walls of an eroded dyke some 40 feet deep with perpendicular walls. There are two of these deep gorges – the top section is the deepest and most spectacular, but there is a shorter narrower section even closer to the road, both fine illustrations of Mull's volcanic history.

22. MacKinnon's Cave

2 miles

A short but energetic walk with a little scrambling in places. As the cave is only accessible from below half-tide, it is essential to check the tide-tables for the day to avoid a wasted journey..........or being cut off. You should also take a torch (no daylight penetrates the innermost recesses of the cave) and keep your dog on a lead till through the gate at the top of the cliffs.

Leave the B8035 just beyond the Gribun rocks where the road begins to climb into Glen Seilisdeir, and go down the farm road. Park the car just short of the cattle grid at Balmeanach and continue up to the farm buildings, bearing left as indicated by a sign to skirt the outbuildings and pass through a gate. Leave the track as soon as it starts to bend to the left and keep above the fence to your right, following it across the field to the top of the cliffs. Dogs must be kept on a lead across this field. A small gate a little to the left of the corner of the field gives access to the shore. A winding track leads downwards and a short quarter-mile along a coast of increasing drama brings you to the cave. Everything here is on a grand scale including the flotsam – there are some huge logs, part of a cargo which floated in the sea for some time and were the subject of a securité warning to shipping before they came ashore. Stick to the top of the beach for the easier walking. Just before the cave there is a waterfall and an area of large, tilted slabs.

Measuring just over 500 feet, MacKinnon's cave is reckoned to be the deepest in the islands. Boswell and Johnson visited it on their tour in 1773. As befitted eighteenth century inquirers, they measured it painstakingly – and with surprising accuracy, considering that their measuring instrument was a walking stick and they only had one candle. They were not, however,

impressed by the legend associated with the cave. The story goes that a group of people headed by a piper went into the cave never to return. Only the piper's dog returned some hours later, crazed with fear and – the most terrible detail of all – without a hair on its body. Go quietly and perhaps you will hear the ghostly wail of the pipes. The return from the cave must be made by the same route, taking time to admire the cliff scenery and the view out to Staffa.

23. Ulva

Ferry to Ulva (On demand when you turn up)
Monday to Friday 9 am to 5 pm all year
Sundays June to September only
Closed every Saturday

Ulva is a private island off the west side of Mull and is a wonderful place for walking – there are no cars, just occasional farm vehicles. There is a rare feeling of remoteness and the very varied landscape makes Ulva a place that is different from other islands.

There are many walks on Ulva, well signposted by the owners of the island, and all fully described in their own guide *The Isle of Ulva*. This walk is one of the most interesting and a good introduction to the other routes of varying length and character. Start at The Boathouse, where there is a small museum and interpretative display, and walk up the track signposted to all routes. At the crossroads turn left to follow the signposts to farm circuit and basalt columns. The track leads through fields where cattle may be grazing until another path forks off to the woodland walk (but save that for your next visit) and soon passes close to Ulva House, a mansion built in the 1950's to replace the older house destroyed by fire during renovations. Of the former house, only the ornamental urns remain.

The track keeps to the edge of a pasture and then you go through a final gate and up on to the open moorland. Above, on the skyline, is the memorial to the Clark family who owned the island until the 1940's. The walk goes through woodland for a stretch then along the cliff tops – look down to see basalt rock columns, not perhaps as grand as those on Staffa, but showing the same hexagonal formation.

The path, clearly marked all the way either by white topped posts, or more subtly, by white painted stones, now heads inland and across an open valley. Up on the right can be seen a cave, known as Livingstone's cave because the grandparents of the famous African explorer and missionary lived here for a short time. The cave is being excavated by archaeologists who have found interesting evidence of very early use – perhaps as early as 8,000 years ago in the Mesolithic period.

After the cave, continue across the burn and up to a ruined village where Livingstone's grandparents were supposed to have lived once they had built their house. This village is typical of the old Ulva villages of which, in pre-clearance times, there were sixteen. Most families would have had a cow for milk and crowdie, perhaps a share in a boat for fishing and grew crops of oats and potatoes. You can still see the ridges of the cultivation strips. Another famous son of Ulva, Lachlan Macquarie, "father of Australia" was believed to have been born in the nearby village of Ormaig. *Lachlan Macquarie, from Mull to Australia* gives a good account of his life and other sites associated with him. To continue the walk follow the path, climbing up through old birch woods then dropping down to join a track. Close to this junction you can see a solitary standing stone in a field – for many years lying recumbent, it has been re-erected and is an imposing example with its sharp pointed top.

The last part of the route is on an unsurfaced road back to the farm steadings – a choice can be made here to go right for the most direct route back to the ferry, or left to take a detour and visit the Telford Church built in 1828. Inside is an outstanding example of an early pulpit with a sounding board (the roof above the minister's head which helped reflect and amplify his voice), and a precentor's desk – a precentor leads the unaccompanied singing of the Psalms. The track leads back to the ferry, but before you enjoy a well-earned rest in the tea-room with home-baking or the famous Ulva oysters, pay a visit to Sheila's Cottage, a recreation of a typical thatched house.

Other enjoyable walks on Ulva include a visit to the old graveyard at Kilvickewen past the cruck mill at Ormaig, the ascent of Beinn Chreagach and the long walk to Gometra.

Ferry to Ulva

Other Short Walks on Mull laid out by Forest Enterprise, with small car parks.

Scallastle
This is a pleasant walk not far from the Isle of Mull Hotel in Craignure. It climbs fairly quickly to give some views of the Sound of Mull and then dips down to the Scallastle Burn.

West Ardhu
A gentle stroll through woodland and meadows. Start on the Dervaig to Torloisk hill road, opposite the road to Kengharair farm.

Garmony to Fishnish
A shore and marshland walk waymarked by red-topped posts. Fine coastal scenery with lots of birdlife, and the chance of seeing cetaceans in the South Mull. Picnic sites at both ends of the walk and benches along the way. Start at the carpark across the road from the rugby ground or the picnic area near the Fishnish ferry terminal.

Further Reading

Other publications by Brown & Whittaker are listed on back cover.

General Mull

HMSO: *Argyll 3* (Mull, Tiree, etc) RCAHMS Detailed and specialised.
Ed. Graham Ritchie, *The Archaeology of Argyll*
N. Hesketh, *The Story of Mull and Iona*. History through the pen of an artist
P.A. Macnab, *Mull and Iona and Highways and Byways in Mull*
Alastair de Watteville, *The Isle of Mull*
Hilary Peel, *Isle of Mull, Iona and Staffa*
N. MacLean-Bristol, *Warriors & Priests, Murder under Trust*. MacLean Clan histories.
Charles Maclean, *The Isle of Mull: Placenames, meanings and stories*
James Hunter, *The Making of the Crofting Community*
Jo Currie, *Mull, the Island and its People*
Ann MacKenzie, *Island Voices, tales and traditions of north Mull*
Meg Douglass, *Lost Townships, Silent Voices, Gazetteer of Mull settlements.*
Mary Lovell, *The Mitford Girls*

Natural History Reference Books

J. E. Richey, *The Tertiary Volcanic Districts*
C. H. Emeleus & B. R. Bell, *The Paleogene Volcanic Districts of Scotland.*
R. Jones, *Mull in the Making*. Geology of Mull
David Stephenson, *Mull and Iona, a landscape fashioned by geology.*
R. Fitter, A. Fitter, & M. Blamey, *The Wild Flowers of Britain & Northern Europe*
A. C. Jermy and J. C. Crabbe, *The Island of Mull, Flora*. Detailed and specialised
Mullarney, Svensson, et al, *Collins Bird Guide*
P. Hayman, *Birdwatchers Pocket Guide*. Slim format pocket guide
Mike Madders & Philip Snow, *Birds of Mull*
Mull Bird Report, published annually
Collins Pocket Guides, *Seashore, Trees, Insects, etc*
Whittet Guides: *Otters, Deer, Eagles, Puffins, Seals, Whales*
Larousse Pocket Guides

Novels and Films

Annabel Carothers, *Kilcaraig*. Family saga of three generations of Mull landowners.
Elizabeth Luard, *Emerald*. Counterfactual historical novel of Wallis Simpson's daughter.
Jessica Stirling, *The Island Wife, The Wind from the Hills, the Strawberry Season*. A saga of Mull in the clearances
Mary Stewart, *Stormy Petrel*
Ken Follet, *The Eye of the Needle*. A film based on the book starred Donald Sutherland and Kate Nelligan.
Archie Roy, *Sable Night*. Supernatural thriller set on Mull
Alastair MacLean, *When Eight Bells Toll*, starring Anthony Hopkins

Relevant to specific walks (walk nos in brackets)

J. Howard and A. Jones, *The Isle of Ulva* (23)
Samuel Johnson and James Boswell, *Journey to the Western Islands of Scotland and Journal of a Tour to the Hebrides* (23)
Jackie le May, *Ardmeanach, a Hidden Corner of Mull* (22)
Richard Baker, *The Terror of Tobermory* (1-5)
Alastair Dunnett, *The Canoe Boys* (13)

Other walking guides

SMC: *The Munros, The Corbetts, The Islands of Scotland including Skye*